Praise for Wayne F. Burke:

"*Black Summer* by Wayne F. Burke is more than a book of poetry. It is an experience to be lived and relived. Burke taps into our most shared experiences of humanity. His conversational verse entices the reader to continue following the exploits of this wandering everyman who searches, yearns for definition, only to find definitions lacking. But the road is all-encompassing. This book is for lovers of a good story, a good life, and is a roadmap for all of us who often find ourselves on the shoulder of life's highway."

– James Benger, author of *From the Back*

"Poems as funny and as tragic as could ever be imagined—from a lifetime of REAL experience in the REAL world."

-Howard Frank Mosher, author, *A Stranger In The Kingdom.*

"A great book that exposes the victories and defeats of being a man without any expectation of pretentious applause."

-Dan Provost, *Darting in and out*

More Praise for Wayne F. Burke:

"Wayne F. Burke is 65 (going on 66) years old. He reminds me a little of Ed Galing, who wrote poems into his 90's. When I used to see Galing in a publication I always read his poems first not because he was old but because I knew he wouldn't bullshit me. I knew there would be no slickness or pretentiousness, no metaphors stretched out so far you forgot where they started, no look-at-me-being-a-poet, pat me on the head, junk. Just a sensitive, sometimes fucked-up, lonely person writing about the moments of his life."

-Mather Schneider

"Burke jolts his reader into a state of awareness—one of the high aims of all art."

-Arthur Hoyle, author, *The Unknown Henry Miller*.

BLACK SUMMER
New & Selected Poems

Poems by Wayne F. Burke

Kung Fu Treachery Press
Rancho Cucamonga, CA

Copyright © Wayne F. Burke, 2021
First Edition: 1 3 5 7 9 10 8 6 4 2
ISBN: 978-1-952411-57-1
LCCN: 2021932858

Cover art: Jon Lee Grafton
Author photo: Wayne F. Burke
All rights reserved. No part of this publication may be reproduced or transmitted in any form or by any means, electronic or mechanical, including photocopying, recording or by info retrieval system, without prior written permission from the author.

The Author Would Like To Thank As Well As Acknowledge The Following Publications For Having Previously Published Some Of The Poems In This Volume:

'Haiku' Published By *Haikuniverse*; 'Little God,' And 'New Kid' By *Down In The Dirt*; 'Spartacus' By *The Literary Yard*; 'Famous,' 'Wife-Beater' And 'Scars' By *Lummox Anthology*; 'Ants' By *As It Ought To Be*; 'Dharma Bums' And 'Poets' By *Cajun Mutt Press*; 'Camp' By *Unlikely Stories*; 'Pearl Diver' And 'Black Summer' By *Yellow Mama*; 'Probation Officer' By *The Rye Whiskey Review*; 'Blondi' By *Under The Bleachers*; 'Hail Mary,' 'Her,' And 'Chowder' By *1870*; 'First Book' And 'Blow Me' By *Beatnik Cowboy*; 'I Know Rainy Nights' By *Ink Sweat & Tears*; 'Never Had A Room' By *Bluestem*; '86'D' And 'Lights' By *The Commonline Journal*; 'The Long Walk' And 'The Chelsea Jail' By *Visions And Voices*; 'Cooked' By *Industry Night*; 'Punks' By *Red Savina*; Tanka By *American Tanka*; 'Stabbed' And 'A Lark Up The Nose Of Time' By *Bareback Review*; 'Moider' By *Rain*; 'Poison Gas' And 'Savior' By *The Screech Owl*; 'Schwartzie' By *Scarlet Leaf Review*; 'Bomber' By *The Bees Are Dead*; 'Beach' And 'The Struggle' By *Paper And Ink Zine*; 'Posse' By *Loch Raven Review*; 'Twilight' By *The Stray Branch*; 'How Did I Love Thee' By *The Rat's Ass*; 'Melville' By *Duane's Poe Tree*; 'Math' By *The Pangolin Review*; 'Roughneck,' 'The Minutemen,' And 'R.I.P.' By *Riverbabble*; 'Streetlights' By *Chiron Review*; 'Eclipse' By *Ramingo's Porch*; 'Sweat & Leather' And 'Fat Bastard' By *Meat For Tea*; 'Rusty' By *The Two-Five*; 'Max' By *"The Song Is..."*; 'Another Day' By *Thirteen Myna Birds*; "Old Buddy' And 'Railroad Tracks' By *Lost Coast Review*; 'Monkey's Uncle' By *The Periphery*; 'The Joint' By *Zombie Logic*; 'Stabbed' By *Locust Magazine*; 'Sunday' By *In Between Hangovers*; 'Wave' By *Versewrights*; 'Morning Glory' By *Dissident Voice*; 'Ascension' By *Miller's Pond*; 'Seat 27-B' By *Crack The Spine*; 'Alone' By *Ricochet*; 'Dogs' By *Dirty Chai*; 'Hard-Boiled' By *Fuck Fiction*, 'Labor' By *Heroin Love Songs*; 'Evil World,' And 'Cards,' By *Terror House Magazine*; "Pricks" And "March 17" By *The Black Shamrock*, 'Obviously' By *The Dope Fiend Daily*.

TABLE OF CONTENTS

Little God / 1

New Kid / 2

Spartacus / 3

Relatives / 5

Ants / 6

a guy on the street / 7

Camp / 8

Dharma Bum / 9

Black Summer / 10

Closing Time / 12

Pearl Diver / 14

Fish-Oh-Lay / 15

fruit-scented woman leaves / 17

Probation Officer / 18

Blondie / 19

Chowder / 20

Her / 22

Hail Mary / 23

Like Tears / 24

5$ / 26

The Space / 27

The Train Whistle / 28

Famous / 29

A Poem / 31

Labor / 32

First Book / 33

I Know Rainy Nights / 34

The Struggle / 35

pigeons flying off the lawn / 36

Cards / 37

Obviously / 39

Evil World / 40

Pricks / 43

March 17 / 44

Morning Glory / 46

Last Kiss / 49

Never Had a Room / 50

Hot Summer / 51

A Cute Little Thing / 52

86'd / 53

The Chelsea Jail / 55

Ascension / 58

Cooked / 60

The Long Walk / 61

Punks / 63

Sunday / 65

The Irish Sea / 67

another email from
   Olive Garden-- / 68

zen he went to the market / 68

ocean waves / 69

Palm Sunday / 69

Stabbed / 73

Showdown / 74

In Praise Of / 76

Old Buddy / 77

Fruit of the Loom / 78

Railroad Tracks / 79

Seat 27-B / 80

A Lark Up the Nose of Time / 81

Doughnuts / 83

Stress / 84

Visitors / 85

Dogs / 86

Hard-Boiled / 87

Monkey's Uncle / 88

Alone / 89

leave the Driftwood Motel / 90

at the dinner table / 90

my jacket / 91

walk with my hands / 91

Dickhead / 92

Turkey / 97

Chipper / 99

Naked / 100

Wife-Beater / 102

Paddy Wagon / 103

Moider / 105

Savior / 106

Poison Gas / 107

The Girl and the Greek / 108

Water / 109

Rights / 110

NORTH / 111

Jackass / 112

Same-O / 113

Hi-Ho! / 114

The Fix / 115

Fat Bastard / 119

Posse / 121

Beach / 123

Bomber / 124

Schwartzie / 125

The Joint / 127

Lights / 128

Scars / 130

Twilight / 131

Prayer / 132

How Did I Love Thee? / 133

Reasons / 134

Black-Out / 135

Advice / 136

Ramrod / 139

Ramrod on the Avenue / 141

Excalibur / 145

Melville / 147

Math / 148

Wave / 150

Fate / 152

Plunkett Junior High School / 153

Roughneck / 155

The Minutemen / 157
Max / 161
Rusty / 163
Happy Birthday / 167
Raccoon / 170
Bat Man / 172
Gold / 174
R. I. P. / 175
Eclipse / 176
Ice Cream / 178
Sweat & Leather / 179
Puke / 180
Streetlights / 181
Linebacker / 182
Geek / 184
Slip / 186
Suspect / 189
Larry / 191
Polio / 195
Palmer Method / 196
100 pounds / 197
Prepositioned / 198
Farm / 199
Van Gogh / 201
Pollock / 204
Poets / 206
Another Day / 208
I Write For the Factory Workers / 209
Blow Me / 211

BLACK SUMMER

fallen leaves the color of
the manila envelopes
I slip poems into and bid adieu

Dedicated to the Three Jewels: BUDDHA, SANGHA, and DHARMA

Little God

it was a murderously hot afternoon
in the
upstairs bedroom
where I squashed flies against the
window, using
a rolled newspaper, their
guts protruding through the
squares of the window screen;
they had to die, it was time
I had decreed--
the dumb and ugly flies would long remember the
day and
me
their massacre at Bitter Creek
their body parts spread in the
trough of the window, I made sure
none survived to
seek vengeance, as if
they could, ha
ha
a hot breeze
like from an oven
blew across my face.

New Kid

the new kid in school looked tough
had a dirty face
and cussed--
he came from the "Welfare House" across the
highway of death
and he scared me
a little
I was leery
wondered why he seemed to hate
my guts
he chased me down Howling Avenue
after school
I banked the corner onto my street
and thought myself safe
but he caught hold and
we wrestled on the
Carnazola's front lawn
he got me in a head-lock
hard to break--
Susie Brown walked up the
street, books under her arm
I finally broke the hold and
ran--
later, Susie told me that
I had been smart to run
but
I did not think so--
in fact, I hated myself for doing it
and hated her too.

Spartacus

I sit in the cushioned chair in the
semi-darkness of the theater, ornate
to my ten year old eyes
and am hit on the head
by a JUICY FRUIT thrown
by a fat kid
behind me
I stand and walk to him
ask did he throw it
yeah
what you going to do about it?
His ghoulish face lit by the
light of "The Vikings" on the
big screen, I hit him and
he sits down
as the Vikings climb the
castle walls…
The theater manager mister taps
me on the shoulder
motions me to follow
up the aisle
his office
walls of movie posters
he asks my father's phone number
he does not have one
how come?
Because he is dead.

Oh.
He asks my mother's number
she is dead too
he demands to know who I live with
and I tell him--
he asks if my grandfather will come and
pick me up
he is in the hospital
he says go back to your seat
and behave
yes I will
I get back
to my seat
just in time
for the 2nd feature
SPARTACUS.

Relatives

12 years old and
sitting in the yard
wondering why the relatives
never stop by
say "hi" or take us, my
brother and me, for a ride?
They know we have nowhere to go
and nothing much to do; know
we have no money and
no way to make any
except to steal from the
purse Grandma keeps locked
inside a drawer of iron...
We play board games, grow bored
with one another, have a fist-fight
while waiting for a car--
any goddamn car--
to arrive.

Ants

no one to play with or
talk to, nothing
I know to do, a hot summer afternoon
I wandered into the Larson's yard next door
sat on their walkway and
watched ants come up out the
cracks and ant hills
a flood of them spreading
across the plain of the
walk, and then
other ants, with wings
flew down from the blue sky
in squadrons,
a blitzkrieg attack--
a mighty struggle began,
ferocious as Hastings or
Waterloo--
the Queen of the wingless crew
rolled over her winged foe
like a tank
the dead and dismembered piled
as the battle raged and the
afternoon slid into shadow:
I did not hear
my grandmother
the first time she called
me
in to supper.

a guy on the street
who looks like me:
I clench my fists
in case he tries to
get tough

Camp

wish I had gone to ART CAMP
instead of FOOTBALL,
five of us guys
from the team
in the woods of New Hampshire
some college campus
I never did get the name of;
we had water-fights in the dorm
and I had to hide under a bed
to avoid being caught
by the proctor;
I found a paperback book in the
closet, CANDY
and read it while
holding the book in one hand
and listening for my roommates or
whomever...
Someone set up a meeting with girls
from another camp,
my cousin did the talking
he was good at that,
I was bashful and
tongue-tied around girls--
the next day during scrimmage
I intercepted a pass
and coach gave me an "attaboy"
plus a pat on the back--
something he would not have done
had I shown him a work of art.

Dharma Bum

I filled a backpack with stuff
mostly books, plus
a Bowie knife with 8-inch blade
for in case of trouble
whenever I hitch hiked
but I never did have
that much trouble
though got creeped-out
once
by a bullet-headed guy who
after picking me up
said "I got a gun under the seat,"
and I said "oh yea?"
And he said "yea."
And I said "I got a knife in my pack."
And he did not reply
and we drove along
in silence
to the next exit
where
I asked to get out
even though
I was going
much
further.

Black Summer

I borrowed money from
whomever
would lend it to me
and without thought of
ever paying anyone
back:
I was living the Henry Miller
creed:
"I please myself."
TROPIC OF CANCER my Bible,
it gave me license to screw
whomever, left and
right:
I sought liberation from convention
and restraint;
my cronies did not understand me
but
so what?
My apotheosis I thought imminent
elevation into the pantheon of
great artists only a matter of time.
I fought against prudery and
the bourgeoisie,
against the 8-hour workday and
the 5-day work week…
I hung around bar rooms, mooching
drinks, and

giving advice to the
barflies
who, I knew
would be better off, happier
if only they would or could be
more like me: more like "Henry Miller"
too, whoever
he.

Closing Time

and George, the bartender
shuts me off
and I throw my handful of coins
down behind the bar
and some guy
a stranger in town
cracks wise and
I try and sucker-punch him
but miss
and he hits me twice as
two of his friends grab my arms
and the guy bashes a billiard-ball down
on my skull--
"fuck this" I say's to myself and
throw both guys off
as WHOOSH
WHOOSH my buddy Leno with
a pool cue, swinging it like
a baseball bat
breaks the billiard-ball guy's arm
as a cop
runs in
spraying mace from
a can, and
everyone, six of us--
are brought to the
Police Station where

the cops let me sleep
in a bed in the break room
instead of in a cell
because
my Uncle
is Mayor of the
rinky-dink town.

Pearl Diver

washing dishes at the Olympia Diner
across the street from the
college I live at, and
sometimes attend classes;
high on black beauties, Friday nights
after the bars close, lugging
buckets of dishes from
front to back for the owner
John Papalopulopulopulopulous
who works eighty hours a week
calls me "lazy American" because
I do not sweep deeply enough under the
counters...His nephew, the "head" dishwasher
tries to boss me; the little prick
can do no wrong in his Uncle's eyes; take
hour-long breaks, make wise-guy remarks--
one Saturday the cigarette machine is found empty
of coins and butts, and
the cops pick the nephew up
but
the Uncle will not prosecute or even fire the
kid, because
I guess
blood is thicker than dish water.

Fish-Oh-Lay

the dim lights of a MCDONALD's
at 2 AM.
in Rutland, Vermont
I order a sandwich but
next window empty
so I park my car, get out
no one around, and
the front door locked;
I return to the window
where
a car
stopped
waiting
I tell the driver I am waiting
too
a guy in the passenger seat
tells me, "I am going to RIP your head off,"
he fumbles with the door handle
"no, no, stay..." the driver says.
The drunk glares, glassy eyes at half-mast:
he pissed-off, spent all his money
in a bar and
could not make a girl,
now being driven home
to sleep alone
in a drunken bed
"rip your head off," he says

"no, no..." the
guy with my food shows
and I skedaddle
wondering
what
would have happened
if the drunk got that door open?

fruit-scented woman leaves
an orchard behind her, what
variety is she, really?

drooping heads of sunflowers
bowing
to the inevitable

Probation Officer

she went out to the Club, and
got drunk, and
blacked-out and
came-to in her bed
in the morning
lying beside a guy,
wearing an ankle bracelet,
whom she did not know--
he said his name was Fred
or Ed
or Ned
and after smoking a cigarette, she
cooked some eggs
but there was no time to eat
because Fred
or Ned or Ed
needed a ride
to go
meet
his P.O.

Blondie

I was putting the stick to Eva Braun
last night, her
head banging the head-board of the
bed, legs of the
bed lifting and
thumping the floor:
"Ja! Ja! Ja!" Eva said.
Suddenly, the door swung open and
Shitler's dog ran in
and bit me on the ass--
"No Blondie!" Eva screamed. "Bad dog!"
I hopped off and
Blondi hopped-on
and as I left
I heard the bed
start thumping
again.

Chowder

I stared into her soft brown eyes
and told lies
she believed;
a nice girl, from
a nice Mid-Western family
she sat on my bed
as I undressed
not caring if
what I was about to do
was wrong
not caring that I was the devil's spawn
with horns on my crown--
my cock
like a truncheon
hung down to my knees--
she stared at it, her
lips parted, and
as soon as I laid down
she went to work
sucking and
slurping
drool running out her mouth
stopping once
to apologize for being loud
("that's alright")
I went off
like a fire hose

and she
gobble
gobble
and swallow.

Her

I think of her
now and then
since I threw her
out--
think of her standing
before me, her
blouse undone and
one tit hung
like a bread loaf
to her belly, and
she asking me
for a hug
which I would not give
because
I could not stand
her vapid presence,
her senseless chatter,
and wanted her gone
far away, and
was afraid that
if I gave
she might
stay forever.

Hail Mary

I told the girl who gave me
a ride home from the
bar to pull into the
parking lot next door
to where I lived, she said
"what for?"
I said "so we can make-out."
She said "but I do not even know you."
I said "oh yea" and
got out of the car
and walked into the
apartment, brightly lit
my grandmother sitting in her chair
saying her rosary
loudly
like a chant
on and on
until
I could barely stand the
sound of her voice.

Like Tears

I lived in a room in a Kenmore Square hotel
Boston, Massachusetts
ten X ten
with a view
the right field corner of
Fenway Park
I felt lonely
could not make the grade
or even a friend out of one
of the million people around me--
I walked the streets
block after block
one night it began to rain
and I did not care
a torrential downpour
across the Common
down Boylston Street
to Copley Square
the rain down my neck
down my back
I came to a building
festively lit
three girls ran out
laughing and
one ran up to me and
took my face in her hands
and then a closer look

UGH she said,
pulled back, and ran
squealing,
through the rain.

5$

she comes across the
parking lot calling
to me: "Sir! Sir!"
Sunglasses on pancake make-up
face (to hide the zits?)
she says she out of gas
her kids miles away
her husband pissed
her ATM card rejected by the machine
won't I give her five dollars for
gasoline?
A little too hysterical to
believe, but
not a bad acting job, if that…
Actress with a crack problem?
Crack-head with an acting problem?
Hard to say.
Oh well, only five dollars, a drop
in the bucket
for a rich fuck
like me.

The Space

below the bedclothes
the Cave of Love
where the two of us
burrowed in warmth and
comfort
away from the rest of the
world, whose only contribution
to our love-making
the headlights of their cars
flashing
blinking once or twice on the
white walls
then leaving us
forever
in the dark
again.

The
train
whistle
blows
a loud hello,
a soft so long:
a clarion call
clear
&
shrill
up
&
down
the
line.

Famous
for M.R.

I asked the famous poet to read
my poems
and he did
and then
arranged to meet me
in the cafeteria
where we sat in a booth
across from one another
and he looked down at my manuscript as
he spoke, his black bangs
over-hanging his face, and
never looking up, not
once, until the
end and
then
I wished he would look back down
again
because
something in his eyes,
anguish of some kind
I could not bear to look at--
he was known as the poet of loneliness and
was married to the poetess of bereavement.
Before leaving, I asked what he really thought of
my things, and
he said,
well

they are all on the surface
no depth to them;
read other things beside literature, he suggested
like "Kramer's book on aesthetics."
I thanked him and he left.

I was the poet of surfaceness.

A Poem

    sitting in a bar room nursing a bitter-tasting
    beer when
    Mahoney, whom I had not seen in
    a coon's age, drops onto the stool
    beside me:
    pale blue eyes of regard, Anglo-face
    bush of curly hair
    and beard:
    says he has been through every bookstore and
    bar room in Cambridge looking for me: says
    "what happened to your face?"
    I tell him of my being beaten in a bar; tell
    him I am going back there with a machine-gun.
    He asks "so what else is new?"
    I pull a sheet of paper from my pocket and
    he reads the words typed on it.
    "Best poem you ever wrote," he says.
    I take another swallow of beer--
    it tastes good.

Labor

first time in years
no labor for me
on Labor Day
I am free of the
factory and
looking forward to collecting
social security checks
unless they are
kept or
canceled by the
scamboogah in Washington
then I will go back
to work:
running a cash register at the
supermarket or
sweeping up over by the
cigarette machine, I do not know
what or
where
or care much
today, because
today I am working
on my tan.

First Book

since my first book was published
I feel as if I have grown
an inch or two,
added an additional foot to my
intestines;
more hair,
harder fingernails,
a darker shadow;
the future has more substance
to it, I want to hurry it
into existence;
but I fear
too
that it will all end
abruptly and
I will be on my back
in a hospital bed
in Marseilles or
elsewhere
and still
unilluminated.

I Know Rainy Nights

the wet cold touch
the splatter
and drip
in wind swept
mist
and black
as pitch
streets
lit by red and
green
scrawls
and torches of
scalding headlights.

The Struggle

if I had a beard
I could stroke it;
one like Uncle Ho Chi Minh
had,
wispy gray;
I could wrap strands
about my finger
and contemplate how to
continue the struggle
against the imperialists and
other bastards,
fighting not
to win
(not immediately, anyway)
but to keep on
for as long as I can--
keep trying
until
conditions change,
or not--
keep trying,
anyway.

pigeons flying off the lawn
a round of applause
I did nothing to deserve

Cards

2 kids on the
sidewalk, the
bigger one says
"hey! You want to buy
some flowers?"
"Flowers?" I say.
"No! Cards. Football and
baseball cards."
The smaller guy carries
a plastic box full
I tell them I used
to have stacks, but
like a fool, threw them
away--
they are not interested in what
I used to do
the bigger says
"you want to buy one or
not?"
I suggest they take the
cards to the GAME Store
the smaller guys says
"the pawn shop."
Cars line up at the
crosswalk as
we talk,
I say the older cards
could be valuable--

they already know
that, and
turn their backs to me
and start across--
"good luck," I call
but they do not respond
probably because
I did not buy a
card.

Obviously

Almost get run into by
a silver SUV shooting through the
parking lot--
"where are you going?" I shout
"do you know?"
The jackass pulls up
in front of the bank.
I hope he tries to start something.
I hope not.
Blue sky, lighter above the
ridge line than
higher up, or
is this an illusion?
I walk through the smell of
the pizza parlor (regret being
on a diet), halfway
across the street
a truck, nose stuck over the
crosswalk: "you know you are on the
crosswalk?"
"Tell me the obvious!" says
the joker (wearing a MAGA
ball cap).

Obvious or not: wtf?

Evil World

I get a call from "amazon"
because my account "hacked"
with a 400$ charge for
an item I did not order
a guy with an Indian accent, tells me
bring up my bank account on-line
he will put the 400$ back
I say "OK" and
bring the account up
and he puts 400$ in
says "see?" But I see
4400$ not 400$
"oh no!" he says
says he made an error
says he will lose his job
unless I send him back the
4000$, I tell him not to worry,
poor guy, I will send him a check
if he provides an address.
He thanks me, says
he is having a "bad day"
I can relate, I know what
those days are like, poor
guy, he says he needs the
money right away, will
I transfer to his bank account?

Sure I will. He helps me through the
paperwork and I send, but
my bank declines to pay
because his bank in
a "sanctioned" foreign country;
I tell my bank send anyway
and the poor guy and I
resend, but
declined again; he
suggests a bank in a different
country and we go through the
process again, and send, but
again, my bank declines to pay--
my "friend" has another idea
but I say I am sick of sending
and am going to go downtown to
my bank and straighten things
out, he begs me not to, "please!
Just two more minutes!" I say
"alright," and give him two, then
two times two, then hang-up the
phone and drive to my bank, wondering
on the way, if something screwy about
the deal…
The bank teller listens to me for
less than a minute before running me
to the manager who
swings into action and
saves my money

(a lot more than 4000$).
The demon had almost caught me
in his crocodile-mouth;
had almost tasted the sum of
my account.

Pricks

I walked upstream through the
woods, among the trees
and rocks
to a quiet place
below the falls
I took my pants off
and sat
in the sun
I was having a herpes attack
boils on my dick
and thought the sun
might fix me up a little
as I listened to the river
flow
THWAK
a rock
ricocheted off a boulder
thrown down from above
some little bastard
his mongoloid head on top the
hillside
I wrestled my pants on
and began the steep climb
but soon
gave up, because
my dick hurt
plus
the little prick long gone.

March 17

how green the grass of
Saint Stephen's Green
next to a pub
where I drank six Irish whiskeys
six Guinness Stout, walked out
and boarded the Dublin-Drumcondra bus
standing room only
I fell and
was lifted up as
the bus
spun out of control
and I lurched
seat to seat
among smiling people
having fun; I crashed into the barrier
and fell out
and wandered pitch black streets
until I found the door
to my sodden basement flat, entered
and passed
out, woke
fully dressed and
to rain
and gloom
outside
plus
the clippity-clop

of a horse
pulling a milk-wagon
through my
head.

Morning Glory

gold folds in the East the
birds glide through
and white rolls West
in pastel-blue
background
and
peeping from
a dusky cloud the
eye of the sun
bright areole
brighter yet the
first rays
across dark roof tops
dark streets
a gold promise of
some kind--
a brighter day--
a new Jerusalem on the horizon:
we cannot get there
because
too far away
but
hell,
let's start walking
anyway
shall we?

From WORDS THAT BURN

Last Kiss

moving from mouth to mouth
kissing every girl in the bar
their boyfriends stand aside and
stare and one bitch has a fit after
I smack her lips and soon I am
outside and lying on the sidewalk
beneath a tree and listening to
wind rustle through the leaves
and if god has a voice that is it
the soothing shush and sibilant
rush, the whispered hush and
sudden gust of exhaled breath
calming me but not enough
because later I climbed the side of
a building and broke in through
a third floor window and came-to
sitting on a bed in a dark room
and heard the footsteps of a giant
outside the door which flew open
to let a cop in who handcuffed me
so tightly the cuffs stayed on my
wrists for years.

Never Had a Room

never had a room of my own until
I was sixteen,
always had a bed;
my two brothers and Uncle
had beds too
in the same room;
my Uncle came home late
stomping up stairs and
falling into bed like a tree trunk
into empty cans;
his snores were like a language
of the deaf and dumb;
in the morning he retched
into the toilet then stomped
to his bed—fat man on Popsicle stick legs--
and sat to put on his gas station uniform
grunting as he bent
to tug up socks.
A bastard he could be
who gave me backhanded slaps
and kicks from size ten shoes and
once whipped me with his belt
as I squirmed on the back yard lawn
howling loud enough for the neighbors and
the world to hear
but they never did.

Hot Summer

after an hour or two
of making-out with
her
I would have a hard-on
like a bar of soap
but she would never
touch it
or even acknowledge
that I had more in
my pocket
than loose change and
when her mother coughed
twice from the living room
it was time for her
to go into the house
and me to walk home
beneath the moon
with my piece
of re-bar
that I never used
for anything that summer
except piss out of.

A Cute Little Thing

she was a cute little thing
with big doe-eyes
and bright smile
and as we kissed one night in front
of the dormitory
after our first date
she squeezed my cock
in her little gloved hand
and the next night
I was sleeping in her room;
she in a bathrobe and chirping
like a bird at dawn
and me high on pot
and without a condom on.
Whenever we sat outside I put my
head into her lap and
she stroked my hair;
it was something nice
bright like her smile
but
when the semester ended
she came to me crying
and hysterical
but would not say why
and I went away
but
remained inside her.

86'd

after working a ten-hour shift in the restaurant
I went to a bar
in Central Square
that served beer in 16 ounce milkshake glasses
and I was on my fourth or fifth
when this broad
with stringy hair, not
washed in a coon's age,
wearing a leather vest--
some type of biker chick--
poked me in the ribs and
said "hey Bub, you are in
my seat," and I said "hey
Sister, go bother someone
else," and she got hold of
my hair and yanked
my head down to the floor
and when she let go
I slapped her across the face
and she went out
on her feet
her eyes two stars--
Raggedy Anne falling back
against the guy next to me...
Someone said "how dare you!"
Someone else sucker-punched me
and I was on the floor

and it was dark
and someone kicked me in the face
and someone kicked me in the ribs
and
luckily I had sat near the door
and made my way through kick after kick
out into the quiet street
as the people from the bar chased me
up the bricks.

The Chelsea Jail

the night of the Ali-Ernie Shavers fight
I was at My Brother's Place
a bar near the Greyhound Bus Station
downtown Boston
and drinking gin & tonics
which were going down smooth
and I decided, after the fight, to take
a bus to Chelsea and
drink in a bar there called 'Heaven's Gate.'
And I was having a good time
feeling-up girls
until a fat guy said
that I had to leave
and I said "why?"
"Because you are pinching the broads' asses,"
he said, "and they do not like it."
He and buddies
hustled me out
into the pouring rain
and cold dark street
and I stood
excluded from life's party,
and brooded until
I decided to go back in
but a half-a-cop at the door
said "you can't come in,"
and I balled my fist

and marked a spot on his
cheekbone where light
from a streetlamp glimmered
and I started to swing
but a voice
far away--
from the Planet Crouton
across the Universe
said "no" and
I walked up the sidewalk
to the corner and a box
in the gutter
with a rock inside
a Dinosaur egg
waiting to be discovered
and I flung the stone--
a Don Drysdale heater--
through the bar room window
then ran
up the rain-slick street
until my shoe came off
and I stopped to pick it up
as two guys from the bar,
wearing softball uniforms,
caught hold of me.
One guy held my arms
the other wailed punches--
Ernie Shavers haymakers
against my head until
the paddy wagon

pulled to the curb and
the two guys and half-a-cop
threw me inside
and I was driven to the Police Station
and booked
and listened to a guy in the next cell
sing "Lord I Want to Go Home"
all night long
while people from the bar
waited outside the jail for me
to be bailed out--
which
did not happen.

Ascension

Gramp, more Claudian than Augustan
died
and unlike Christ
failed to rise
on the 3rd day
or any other--
Uncle Albert, brazen as any
Nero, at the head of the
table
sat wrapped in layers of fat
thick as walls keeping Chinas' in or out:
I ran like a coolie to Uncle's shouts.
Agrippina-Gram limped from stove to
sink to table serving the meat & potato.
My sister gnawed a bone; my brother
impersonated a clam...Uncle, the
Great-Man-of-the-Dinner-Table, ruled with
an iron hand, only his rules changed
like his moods, from black to blacker, and
I was always wrong, crooked somehow
in need of being straightened by a kick
from size ten shoes, or a slap of his calloused
hand--
Gram folded her wooden lap: she bled the
years together and was caught in the groove of a record
going round--

I failed to wipe several different looks off my face.
I had insurrection in mind.
I was Spartacus against the power of Rome
and I lost every time.

Cooked

I was cook at Vagina Pizza in Cambridge, Massachusetts
and one night at end of shift a waitress asked
did I need a place to sleep
and I said "no" and turned my back and walked out
carrying my suitcase and duffel bag—my ball and chain--
and slept in the bus station shelter until a cop woke me
and said "you can't sleep here," and I walked until dawn
while shiny police cruisers running smooth as vacuum cleaners
patrolled the empty streets.

The Long Walk

another MANPOWER job
where they send you out to work
and take half your pay
only it was not a bad job, this one:
mixing paints, putting
the cans into the arms
of a machine and
watching the machine jiggle like
a belly dancer…
I got off at four
and started to hitch hike
but could not get a ride
and all the drivers
looked smug, like bastards, laughing at me, and I thought
"fuck you assholes, I will walk"
my back to the traffic
cars going past at
sixty, the bastards!
I was pissed; even if
a car stopped I would
not get in.
I marched like one of
Caesar's soldiers going
to meet the Gauls,
sweating out my ass;
it was hot, hazy, no
breeze, people moved
out of my way, I must not have looked normal.

I was not normal.
I was pissed.
I walked eight miles
back to the place.
A girl who lived in the
apartment asked
how I got back and I said
"I walked."
She had a Mid-Eastern look and
was screwing
a black guy from Detroit who smoked pot and
did not talk.
Me, I was not screwing anyone
except myself.

Punks

standing on the main street of Framingham,
Massachusetts
holding my thumb up
in the air
and watching all the cars in the world
drive by me
and all the drivers look like assholes
to me
and a car goes past with some punks inside
and one punk gives me the middle-finger
and I turn and chase the car
as the punks point and
laugh at me until
their car slows then stops at a red light
and I gain ground
and the smiles of the punks disappear
their eyes widen like doll's eyes
and the car squeals out and
I chase it to the
next light
and the punks in the back seat hop around
like monkeys in a cage
as I close the gap again
and the car shoots ahead
and I chase it to the next red light
which the car blows through
and I give up,

out of breath
still pissed
but not really
about
a bunch of punks.

Sunday

Sunday morning walking down O'Connell Street
in Dublin, Ireland
a man beside me
his face red
pork pie cap on
he vomits into the gutter as
church-goers in their Sunday best,
ties and suits and gingham dresses,
all the shops closed
the Liffey River flows, but barely, like
a mud puddle, one that Joyce
made such a song and dance about--
dirty kids on the bridge say mister mister
give us pence!
Upheld hands like pigeons,
ragged clothes
I throw some crumbs
and they scramble, run--
a swan spreads its wings over the river
and I fly too
though feeling disreputable
in my jeans, lumberjack shirt
and with my hangover
I walk backstreets
and am followed by a pair of mean-looking sons of Erin
I lose in an alley
sweating into my shirt until

I come back out onto O'Connell
and the wee freckle-faced red-haired folk
parade in their suits
on the Irish day of partial sanity.

The Irish Sea

The elevator goes up & down
as the ferry boat bobs
like a bar of soap
in a bathtub
and ocean waves rise to walls
and fall in avalanches--
smoke from my cigar is whipped away
like ghostly wraiths
to the stern
a football field away
from where I stand at the rail
of this steel toy vessel,
play thing of the sea,
and try to see into the future
which is all gray-green water
rising to a hillside
cascading to a plain
up-see-doosey and down again
it is not time for a swim
my knees go weak with the thought:
I sink like the Titanic into the briny salt
sea of myself.

another email from
Olive Garden--
what does she want now?

zen he went to the market
zen he came home

ocean waves of
stuporous languor--
the maid sweeps the sun deck

Palm Sunday--
my brother and I
whip each other with palms

From DICKHEAD

Stabbed

I told her while we were
lying in bed:
told her it was over.
She started to weep and
I wanted to comfort her
but could not, would not
and got up and went out
to the kitchen
and poured myself a drink
and she came out of the room
a little later
dry-eyed
and without any clothes on
but not really naked
and said "if I had a knife
when you told me
I'd of stabbed you"
and how glad I was
then
that I had told her in bed
and not in a restaurant.

Showdown

as I lifted weights in the cellar
I listened to the floor boards overhead
creak
from the weight of my Uncle's feet;
I thought of my fist
landing SPLAT in the middle
of his fat face.
His days as boss man
were past
and he knew it too;
and one morning in the kitchen
as I combed my hair
which I had let grow long
he asked when
I was going to get a haircut
and I said "never"
and he flinched
like he'd been slapped
and stared
black-eyed
with the glare that used to
pin me to the floor like a rabbit
but this time I glared back
and we stood
with the sun burning the roof above
and the years piled up between
us;

and then he turned his head
and with a sick smile
fled
out the door
as gutless
as any other bully
who ever ran.

In Praise Of

the beautiful Shelia O'Ryan
10th grade English teacher
who was from elsewhere
and was flown in with
her long lovely legs dangling
and praised my writing and
read it out loud to the class;
she was graduated from Bryn Mawr
or Smith, summa cum laude, and
could speak Old English, she said
and did we want to hear some?
Sure we did.
All the guys sat up front
and Schlonski, an offensive tackle
kept dropping his pencil to try
and look up her dress
an act I hated him for
because to me
she was special
like a solar eclipse
and her praise something I needed
something I did not get from
anyone else
except coach
who only gave it
when
I knocked someone's head off
onto the field.

Old Buddy

I stopped in to see my old buddy
in the old neighborhood
and
he did not recognize me
because I wore mirror shades
and I thought he might attack
so tore the glasses off and
then we sat in his backyard
which seemed smaller than I remembered
and when he went back into the house
to get me a beer
his mother came out and
looked at me and
said "I wondered who the bald man in the yard was."
My buddy, who lived in the apartment above
his parents, told me
he was divorced after
his wife ran off with his best friend
and that he, my old buddy, had
got religion
and that
the Bible
was the first book he'd ever read
from beginning to end.

Fruit of the Loom

after having had the shit
kicked out of me
in a bar in Central Square
I walked alone
up the sidewalk bricks
toward Harvard and the Charles River.
The few people I met
gave me
a wide berth
after a gawk at my face
which must not have looked
pretty
and I reached the river bank
and took my pants off
then underwear
which I began to wash out
but thought hell with it and
threw them into the swirling dark
where
they were later found by an oarsman
rowing in a regatta
speared at the end of an oar like a white fish
species unknown.

Railroad Tracks

hanging-out on the railroad tracks
with my buddies,
a hippie ex-ski bum
and a psychiatric patient who
once put a bullet from a thirty-ought-six
into the church steeple.
What am I doing on the tracks, I ask myself.
Wasn't I President of my High School class?
Didn't I spend a year at the University?
None of that matters now--
nothing matters except
the pot and
the beer.
Everything else, like
the world situation
for example
is
like us
immaterial.

Seat 27-B

we are at twenty-seven thousand feet
there is an old lady on my right
she is chewing and fidgeting
maybe saying her prayers
she becomes self-conscious when I look
across her to see out the window
on my left is an asshole
with a suit on, Mr. Spic and Span
he looks like the MC on JEOPARDY
he is invisible, does not want to be
touched or looked at or acknowledged
he reads a New York Times
he has taken possession of the armrest
I am stuck
in the middle
without a newspaper
or a prayer.

A Lark Up the Nose of Time

we left Kansas after the
bars closed
Ron and Steve and me
in a station wagon
that I passed-out in
the back of
and woke
below a huge steel arch
high above
like a gate to Heaven
but it was Saint Louis
which we bombed through
all the way to Daytona
and got a hotel room
and sat indoors for three days
as
hurricane winds drove white sea horses
to shore and
branches of palm trees whirled
like broken helicopter blades…
On day four we got sun burned
and drunk
and I was so hungry
that night
I punched-out the Plexi-glass
of a candy machine
and tried to eat a candy bar

old as World War One
and in the morning I woke
wet
from piss
in my bed
and
covered the spot
best I could
and we drove back
out of money
out of smokes
and Ron got ugly
without his fix
and Steve
a born-again liar
told one whopper after
another
all the way to Ottawa.

Doughnuts

I got off work at 3 in the morning
after working another twelve hour shift
and I drove my car
to the P & C Market
where I turned a few doughnuts
on the ice
of the lot
before I parked and
got out
and walked to the door
where some guy,
who stood looking at me, said
"I do not care how old you are,
do not pull doughnuts in the lot"
and I said
"FUCK YOU"
and he blinked behind
his cock-eyed glasses
and I followed him inside
and asked if he'd heard
what I said, but
he did not reply
and I went about my shopping
too tired to
give a shit
or
take any
either.

Stress

woke
feeling stressed
8 AM.
bedroom overcast
the telephone blinking
with a call from work
asking for more hours of
my life
plus a dream
in my head
of me escorting a woman
two girls, two cats
through busy city streets--
a job and one half
and I am beat
and have not even
brushed my teeth
yet.

Visitors

there is a flying saucer
hovering
a big mother
from the Planet Crouton
in galaxy X-10
and with gamma ray guns
enough to destroy the city
but for some reason
they do not
and when a rope is thrown
from the craft
a little man
climbs down
to the street
and goes inside of Dunkin' Donuts
and asks for the restroom key
which they will not give
because he is not
a paying customer.

Dogs

he owed me a shit-load of money
for the dope
but would not pay up
so
one day I climbed the hill
across the street from his house
and lay in the grass
waiting
until the fuck came out
and then I rested the stock
of my thirty-ought-six
on my shoulder
and sited the cross-hairs
and shot
the dog
and that guy
you should have seen him
run--
like a jackrabbit--
and afterward
he started to cough-up
some jack and
I was glad
though
I did feel bad
for that dog.

Hard-Boiled

I handed the clerk my
note
but the dumb bitch
could not read my writing
and looked at me as if
I had two heads
and when I said "hurry up" she
acted like she was waiting for the bus
or something
so
I shot her
and then I shot the manager
who came running out of the office
like a hero
and he died on the floor over by the
pretzels
and I got out of there
thinking
they both died for a hundred bucks each
which was chicken shit
but that clerk
she should have been able to read
better
and that manager
he was just
a jerk.

Monkey's Uncle

they played classical music
to calm the apes
who were intent
upon rape and
mayhem until
they heard Brahms,
then they sat back
and put on the
tuxedos the women
gave them to wear
and the apes went
to the ball smelling
like perfumed frauds
with their hair combed
back and during the
Concerto in E-Minor
sat rapt and only
scratched themselves
during intermission.

Alone

he lived in a back room
of DD's Bar & Grill.
His name was Pete
or Art or Earl
and he had come to town
from somewhere else
long ago.
Aloneness clung to him
like a coat;
alone in a crowd
alone in the street
alone smoking a cigarette
that he cupped in the palm of his hand--
his face was a mask
hammered from stone
and DD rode his ass
if he, Earl or Art or
Pete, did not sweep or
mop fast enough
or clean the glasses
until they shone.

leave the Driftwood Motel
and head somewhere
up the coast

at the dinner table
my sister threatens suicide:
pot roast again

my jacket--
hung by the neck
until Spring

walk with my hands
in my pockets
among the descendants of the Mayflower

Dickhead

sitting in the park
after dark
with my cock out
like a little telescope
looking for submarines--
the park is surrounded with
spotlights and
maybe a few cameras…
I wonder if the vice-squad will show up:

"ALRIGHT BUDDY! What you got there?"

Badges flash:

"Dick out in the park! That's a five-oh-oh-seven! Book him!"

My cock starts to shrink,
retreats like a mole into its hole.

I squint at names of Civil War dead on a plaque.

My cock suddenly stands and salutes:
"suck me suck me," it says.

"Pipe down!" I say
"do you want to get us arrested?"

"Eat shit," my cock says, "and
also—keep your goddamn hands off me."

I zip up.

"I will try," I say
"but no guarantees."

From KNUCKLE SANDWICHES

Turkey

The kids shouted as they
circled me on the
schoolyard play ground
"turkey-gobble-gobble!
"turkey-gobble-gobble!"
It was Thanksgiving:
because I was a "Burke"
I was also a "Berkie"
which some evil kid had
translated to "Turkey,"
a name I disliked--
I was sensitive to slights;
I ran at them and
they scattered
but shouted even louder
a hellish chorus
faces gleeful with malice:
"Turkey-gobble-gobble!"
One kid was slow to move
and I caught him with a punch;
he was in the retarded class
taught in the school basement
it was rumored he had a tapeworm--
we fought it out:
he was tough
and with a head hard as wood;

the fight went on a long time
before he said, "I give."
Afterward, no one called me
"Turkey" again,
not to my face
anyway.

Chipper

I pulled back the rubber band
of the slingshot
and hit the chipmunk
with a rock
and the chipmunk flopped
about on top of
a stone wall
and
to put it out of its misery
I beat it with a stick
but the thing would not
die
and I beat it some more
but
still alive
and I began to cry
and
beat it again
and again
saying "die! Die!"
and finally
it did
and I felt ashamed
of myself
because I knew
then
how badly that chipmunk
like me,
had wanted to live.

Naked

The lion roared into the
hearts of everyone
in the theater
and the movie began,
Elvis, or The Three Stooges, or
once, The Naked Prey
which scared me
Friday night
I had gone to meet
my new Junior High School friend
who did not show
and I sat by myself
in the dark
as half-naked dancing girls
shimmied on the screen
in coming attractions
that did not attract
but terrified me
I felt an aura of evil,
of adult-somethingness
beyond my seventh grade
understanding, and
then the movie
which featured the torture
and mutilation
of white men
who intruded into

darkest Africa,
and I stood up and
went out to the concession
run by the theater-owner's kindly mother
only she was not as kindly as
she was on Saturday afternoons
she seemed Gypsy-like and strange
dressed all in black
and part
of the evil
I had stumbled into
and was in danger
of
somehow
becoming a part of.

Wife-Beater

the jail cell was thin and
long;
I sat at one end
and a wife-beater
at the other.
The wife-beater paced the floor
back and forth;
he was tall and thin and had crazy eyes;
whenever he came near
I stared him down.
I wondered if I would
have to beat on him;
maybe that was why
they put me in there.
I did not care who he had beat;
I had no opinion on his case.
Hell,
I wasn't even married.

Paddy Wagon

running down a dark
rain-slick street
chased by
two big guys from the bar,
my shoe fell off
onto the cobblestones
and I stopped
to pick it up,
because I only owned one pair, and
one of the guys
grabbed me
and pinned my arms
and the other wailed
punches, George Foreman
style, the
bite of the guy's ring on
my scalp, his
fist's flashing past
my face like
my past lives
the beating went on
and on
until the paddy wagon arrived
and the guys and a cop
threw me inside
onto a mat
like the ones they used to use

in gym class in Junior High
and I lay back
as the wagon rattled
and the streetlights flashed through
a screen window
and I recalled how much
I disliked Junior High,
except for gym class.

Moider

a squirrel in the park, plump
7 to 8 inches in height
svelte gray coat
attacked a girl
who later died
and the cops went berserk
guns blasting and
killed two hundred squirrels
but none of the witnesses
to the attack
could positively ID the perp
so the cops put out an APB with
an artist's sketch of
the killer-squirrel
which brought 1000 calls
into the station house
but
as of this writing
the suspect remains at large
possibly
up a tree
or
in some hole in a wall.

Savior

with money from my
McArthur grant
I bought a truck load of AK-47s
and loaded them onto
a rented Boing 747 and
crash-landed the plane
in the Gaza Strip and
started handing the weapons
out the back door
and all the people there
praised my name
and loved me like a savior
except for the Hamas bastards
who did not want me around
to louse-up their martyrdom racket
so kicked my ass
into Egypt
but the Muslim Brotherhood
did not think much of me
either.

Poison Gas

I wrote a letter to
Basher Assad in Syria
asking for
some poison gas
because
I want to use some
on the neighbors
they're all sons a bitches around here
even the parolees across the street,
gas them too
and do the town as well--
a bunch of bastards--
and while I am at it
hell
might as well do myself.

The Girl and the Greek

she was a good girl but
headstrong
had to have her own way
and one day her boss
in the restaurant
underpaid her by ten bucks
and she went and opened the
cash register and
took out a tenner
and the boss
a Greek with a bushy mustache
grabbed her
and I grabbed him
slammed him against a wall
tore the buttons off his shirt
and asked, as
I held him by the throat,
did he want to fuck with someone?
And he said "no"
very humbly and
un-boss like
and I let him go
and then
the girl and me
we went back to our place
because
she wanted to fuck.

Water

cold Army-green river
that Fred slipped into
below the barely opaque
surface that wrote his
death certificate in frothy
curlicues like Arabic
though he was Polish
I think, but do not really
know; he always said hello
like we were best friends
though I did not even know
his last name; he swam
out of the picture frame
and came-up fish gray
on the shore. He wore a suit
jacket and looked Asiatic.
He smoked CAMEL or LUCKY
STRIKES non-filter; had brown
nicotine stains on his fingers.
He spoke so slowly you had
to finish his sentences for him.

Rights

in Cambridge, Massachusetts, outside
The Mug & Muffin Restaurant
a guy wearing a pork pie hat was
singing "Sixteen Tons" for
spare change
as another guy
over by the newspaper kiosk
poured gasoline from a can
over his head then asked passersby for a match
and some jackass gave him one
and some waitress screamed
and the guy with gasoline was
tackled
and as I moved ahead
against a tide of liberals
fleeing
as if for their lives
a girl with terror-stricken eyes
ran into me
as the guy
pinned to the ground
screamed
"I want my rights!"
as if
setting himself on fire
in public
was one.

NORTH

drying October leaves like
clenched fists
holding onto the trees...
I am coming to the end of
Celine's NORTH
his tragic-clown-chronicle
of his post-collabo days when
he, his wife Lilli, his friend and
fellow fascist Le Vig, and
Bebert the cat, also
fascist, fled France and lived as
"Franzosen" in Prussia,
protected by remaining Nazis,
ones not dying in flaming Berlin, 1944.
Quite a trip...the good doctor Destouches...
the racist Celine...his apocalyptic style of
three dots...three Franzosen...they have
kept me company...800 pages...me, alone
in Vermont...I am not complaining...
not at all...just a fact...like the leaves...
dying, clinging to the trees with
my fingertips.

Jackass

trouble at the door of
Dunkin' Donuts:
a guy smiling like a
happy jackass
stands holding the door open
for me
and
when I fail to say
"thank you"
or anything else
his happy face turns to
mud
like the coffee served inside
and he snidely says
"you are welcome!"
To which
I reply
"get bent!"
And all his happiness
disappears into
the uncouth bowl
of jackass
life.

Same-O

got a break:
a week away
from this place,
and now I am back
and see
that
the old dump
has not changed
same characters and places to avoid,
same attitudes of indifference,
same lack of anything approaching liveliness,
same incrustation,
same cracks in the facades;
the train whistle sounds the same,
so do the sirens;
the same amount of staring going on
as before;
same everything, nothing
has changed:
nothing can.

Hi-Ho!

I am the Lone Ranger after
Tonto died
after Silver ran off
after the mills shut down
and the welfare state came around
and chain stores and malls
moved in
and Mom and Pops' moved out
and nobody knows their neighbors
anymore
and heroin became the new
pot
and men started to wear earrings
and women got tattoos on their chests
and the good jobs went overseas
and cities went under
and heroes
like me
could no longer find
work
because nobody trusted a masked man
anymore.

The Fix

It is a nowhere trip
to the starting gate--
your horse has already bolted
so you start to run
the track
and the fucker is endless
and every so often
the horses come around
and run over you
and you get back up
(have to)
and shoot for place or show
because winning has been long forgot
but most of the time the best
you can do
is to keep going,
that's it…
and the race
hell,
it's fixed anyway.

From A LARK UP THE NOSE OF TIME

Fat Bastard

I sailed down the hillside
on my silver saucer
and when the saucer hit the road
I jumped up running
as long-legged Big Louie, lanky
and peanut-headed, chased me;
his eyes squinted in a raisin-face
the white wall of my house down the street
bounced up and down
my rubberized clod-hopper boots
I ran up the drive as
an ice-ball slammed into the side of my face
Big Louie screamed
triumphant; I ran up the frozen porch steps
bawling and
barged into the kitchen
where my Uncle, home from work at the
gas station, stood before the
stove cooking:
"Big Louie hit me!" I shouted
then ducked
in case my Uncle tried to back-hand me
for interrupting his Saturday afternoon:
"get in the car," he growled.
He came out wearing his black Navy pea-coat
and looking like a mitten with a head,
we floated down the white street

snow banks to the push-button windows
of the big Buick
to the skating rink
where Big Louie
his pals
stood in a phalanx
arms crossed on chests,
brave in a group, like
wolves--
my Uncle stepped up to them, short and
round, a svelte 300 pounds
a saturnine face
his leather hand shot out
and Louie fell down, got up
his face red
as a stop sign
he ran
like a deer
loping strides up and over the snowbank
and into the tree line…
My Uncle got back into the car, said
"he will not call me
a 'fat bastard' again--
at least not to my face."

Posse

in 5th grade I beat-up a 6th grader
in the schoolyard
and after school
the 6th grader and
a posse of his friends
chased me and a buddy
around the
neighborhood
until we were treed
like coons
on the roof of the
Burnham's garage
and Mr. Burnham
with half a bag on
screamed at us
get down!
and we did
and the 6th grader
started to beat on my buddy
and I went to his aid
and got beat on
by the rest
until
from the Burnham's block
3 girls ran out
and saved me
because

they afterward
said, the
fight was not fair:
none of us knowing
then
that
nothing is.

Beach

a hot muggy day
no one to play with
all the kids gone
to the beach
Charlie Baguette told me I could go
with him
his family
I ran home for my suit
and when I returned
they had already gone…
I climbed the tree in the yard
and sat
hidden by dinner-plate-sized leaves.
I picked my nose until it bled;
meanwhile, the sky turned milky-white and
I was glad (maybe
the Baguette's would be drowned
in the coming storm).
I climbed down and lay in the
driveway on hot cinder
that felt like sand;
I hoped I got run over.
I watched a bird
a speck
far above
until
it disappeared.

Bomber

the big backyard tree
hard as iron
had soft smooth bark of shallow ridges
I ran my hand over
and pressed my cheek against...
It grew string bean-like pods
a foot long
with pillow feathers inside;
my Uncle said they were watermelon seeds
and I wondered was it a lie
like everything else he said?
Dinner plate-sized leaves hid me
as I sat
high up
in the "bomber's seat"
a branch thick as a tire
that wiggled when I jounced it
and from where
when I was upset
I dropped bombs
on the people below--
one's who deserved them.

Schwartzie

I threw him a pass and the
ball hit him
in the head
he could not catch
all he could do was shoot
he'd spent a lifetime on the court
his father had built
the only Jew
on the team
I asked him how he liked his gefilte fish
and he did not like that
or me;
during practice I blocked his
layups because
he could not jump
only shoot
all he could do
shoot the eyes out, when
we played an all-black high school
he played like a pro
a master of the shvartzers
but against the goyim
he did not have it
tended to choke
and everyone wondered why

I said because he was a Jew
and Jews were no good
I knew
because
my grandmother had told me so.

The Joint

so drunk I could barely stand, Mahoney
held me up
at the bus stop in Cheyenne
after dark
after the bars
with big elk and antelope heads
on the walls
their sightless stars of eyes
and some guy who
said hello
said he remembered me
from being inside the joint--
the bus driver said I could not board
Mahoney spoke silver words
to get us on
I fell asleep in the seat
my head fell on Mahoney's shoulder
he elbowed me
like a punch
and I straightened
awake
for a moment
then went back
into the blackness
and the cell in the joint
where
I had never been.

Lights

we got stopped by cops
in a show of blue light
and a cop told my cousin
"step out of the car" and
made him walk a straight line
touch his toes
then his nose
and my cousin, as
shit-faced as he was
somehow passed the tests
and we drove off
to the Club
where we picked-up two girls
and drove up to the mountain top
with them
and parked;
the wind howled around the car
non-stop
the lights of the town dully glowed
in the valley below;
my cousin and his girl went for a walk.
My girl had bow-legs and
a pig-tail; she
unzipped my pants
then pulled hers off
and straddled me
as I lay back; she

guided me inside of her and
then moved up and down and
lifted off as
I shot and
the wind wailed and
the car rocked
and down below the lights winked
on & off.

Scars

I was back in my hometown
and met a guy
I knew
in a bar
I had not seen him in years
he asked me how
I got the scars
on my face
I did not know they were that
noticeable
I could have told him it was because
I had lived a little
but he would not have understood
because
he had never left town
his face was as unmarked
and smooth
as it had been in High School
where we had been
children
together.

Twilight

she did not come to me
for love
but for help
because she was troubled
had some kind of daddy-problem
I think
said that she
felt "safe" with me
and I wondered why
and if it was a compliment.
She stayed a few days
then went away
after saying she would be back
soon
and I sat on the porch
and waited
a week of afternoons
on a street of third floor
walk-ups and
peaked roofs
and gloomy twilight's
and car headlights few
and far between.

Prayer

after my operation
when I was so sick
and could not get up
out of bed without
tremendous effort and
pain
I prayed as I lay
in the dark of my bedroom:
I prayed to my mother
and to my father
and to Theodore Dreiser
and they helped me
a little
I think, but
the pills helped
more.

How Did I Love Thee?

Let me count the swizzle sticks
and empty bottles
the cocktail shakers
and the olives
the coasters I never used
the glasses I did not bother with
the ice cubes I never wanted
the puddles on the bar
the soggy dollars
the hours
the hours
the stools and chairs
the jukebox
R 7 "Riders on the Storm"
A 4 "Sixteen Tons" by Tennessee Ernie Ford
the ashtrays
the smoking cigarette butts
the pickled eggs and crackers
the Slim Jims
the beer nuts…
I loved you more than the summer days
I glimpsed through the
curtained windows.

Reasons

motel sign like an illuminated
spark plug or
robot that
turns it's head to
look at me
lying on a bed
too hot
to sleep in
no air conditioning
this $65 a night box;
the night drips drop by drop
like sweat from
the ceiling:
I list the reasons
I do not like life
then I fall asleep
and when I wake
take them all back.

Black-Out

I wrote letters from
my rooming house
room while I was
blacked-out; a few
good ones, language spare
and close to the bone;
most gibberish, some
illegible;
never sent them,
wonder where they are.
Long gone, like the
typewriter I used to
write them, like the
friends I wrote to, like
the person who wrote
them.

Advice

burn all bridges
as soon as you cross
them
because you are going to
want to
go back, and
if the bridge
is still intact, you
will.

Believe me, you
will.

From IN DREAMS WE CHASE THE LION

Ramrod

he stood too close to me
in line
at the Winn Dixie
pushing his stuff past me
along the belt
and I accidentally elbowed him in the gut
and he stepped back
and took a swing I blocked with my left arm
and then hit him flush
in the face
broke his nose, I think
and he fell to his knees
and the little woman behind him
screamed
and the store manager and cashier
gathered round the guy
who stayed down, and
I plucked my bags off the counter
and walked out
thinking the peckerwood should have known better
than to crowd me
and that maybe he was from New York
and did not know any better…
Someone gave my license plate number
to the cops
who came by my place
to tell me that

I was banned from Winn Dixie
forever
and I thought
oh well
now I will have to drive an extra ten miles
to the Publix.

Ramrod on the Avenue

they were walking down the street
and up to no good
I could see that
two black guys
one with a hood
the other a red bandanna tied
around his head
the hooded guy walking in and out the road
cars swerving to avoid him
the bandanna walks
right at me
like he cannot see me
and I say "excuse me"
and look into the yellow yolks of his
eyes before
we collide and
he spins on his heels
say's "you white mothafucka!"
The hooded guy comes at me
from the side
and I kick him in the ribs
then doo-rag punches me in the face
and I fall onto the roadside gravel
as hooded guy's boot
comes at my face
and I catch it, jump to my feet
and kick him where it hurts the most

and he falls down
then egg-yolks pulls a knife
about 4 inches long
"you dumb son of a bitch," I say's
as I pull my 10 inch steel blade
and we circle each other
until he lunges
and I stick him in the wrist
and he starts spurting blood
like from a fire hose
and then a passing cop car stops
tires squealing
and the cop jumps out
and handcuffs the hooded guy
then pulls his gun on the other one
spouting blood
"good job Ramrod," the cop says
"we have had our eye on these two,"
he pats me on the back
as I turn to leave
and I think
hell
what will the rest of the day
be like?

From Pt. 2, the NAM.

Excalibur

I had it out with Stumpy
as we sat eating C-rats
in a base camp clearing
on a mountaintop I never
did get the name of.
Elmer said something about
Mama Sahn's and
Stumpy said he was with a girl
he described
and I knew from the description
it was May Ling, my woman
and as I used my P-38 can opener
on a tin of lima beans and ham
(I had traded for with crazy Tex
who likes the eggs and ham)
I felt my blood begin to boil
and told Stumpy that I felt like
sticking my K-bar into his throat
and he said "don't" and that
he would fuck me up
seven ways to Sunday
if I tried
and Elmer told me
cool it man
save it for the Cong
but I was too PO'd to cool it
so stood and walked

out the perimeter
hoping I'd step on a claymore
or else get shot
and I stopped under the canopy of trees
where it was quiet and peaceful-like
and a weird-looking bird
orange and blue with
a Mohawk haircut
swooped down and
started to tweet a song,
the bird's round-shaped bill
like a smile on it's face
and its feet black as if
dipped in ink, and
as it sang a sun beam came through
like the sword of Excalibur
only a sword of peace not war
like some sort of sign, I thought
from who knows what or where
and I calmed suddenly and
decided to forgive and forget Stumpy
and all the rest
for boom-booming with my girl.

Melville

was a queer fish
who flopped around the house
and got on his wife's nerves;
he went to church but
only because she wanted him to, he
did not believe or
disbelieve, he
was a fence-sitter, nominally
Unitarian, who
floundered around in Schopenhauer and
Omar Khayyam; his poetry
cut-topaz, shining but
ungainly; easy
to admire, impossible to love;
he sacrificed his two sons to the
devil of Calvin, one
a suicide the
other a bum;
and he died an ancient Mariner
in the cold bosom of
his wife's love.

Math

Mrs. LaBoy had a talk
with my grandparents
on Parent-Teacher Night
and they came home
frowning
faces nearly ashen
Gramp had me get my math book and
sit
at the kitchen table
where
he said
I would stay all night
or for the rest of my life
if necessary;
he showed me how to do a few problems
then he left
to go to work
and I got my story book out
HOW THE WEST WAS WON
and I was soon
on the trail
with Kit Carson
deep in the Rocky Mountains
and did not hear Gramp
sneak back in through the front door
I only felt the slap
(feel it still)

to the back of my head...
I stuck with math
afterward
but never did get the hang of it, and
never did trust Gramp again
either.

Wave

...the wave breaks over its own breaking
Jorie Graham

a misty Gulf Coast morning,
white-capped waves lolly-gagging
onto shore and
creeping onto the beach
before sliding back
into jade overlap
one wave after another
leaving a stain of
tan on mauve sand
a sort of hem to the slippage
back
until waves meet incoming
out-going
capped
recapped
talking in a megaphoned whisper
and occasional
Clap
out beyond where waves
KABOUSH
the breakers fold
and roll
spreading a white froth
for the lazy stroll
shoreward

and then
retraction
and again the frothy lace
slide and spread
the stain of wetness
and scrum of
newly formed jade wrinkles
slowly advancing
like old age.

Fate

I fell asleep inside the aluminum capsule
moving 600 miles per hour
I always sleep
whenever I fly:
the sleep-inducing jounce and jiggle
the total loss of control
over whether or not we crash and die
or not crash, not die
out of my hands
hopefully the pilot
not high
not ill
not incompetent
did not have too bad a fight
with his wife before boarding
but crash not crash
die not die
I have nothing to do with
either,
I got onto the plane,
that the fateful decision,
I bear the consequences of
whatever.

Plunkett Junior High School

wind-blown snow like dust
up the dresses of the girls
who huddle
like birds
not too close
not too far
from one another
the school bus smells of
exhaust
frog-faced Abboo the Bus Driver
does not respond to
"good morning" or
even "hello"
his exophthalmic eyes see everything
through the rear view mirror:
the wise guys
in the back, the
roadside houses, the
railroad tracks he
stops the bus at:
I look out the window
for signs of life in town
only buildings with black eyes
look back--
one day I will step off the bus
and not get back on, when
will that day come, I wonder

as the gears grind down
and the doors open with a sigh--
the school looks like a fortress
but is really
a prison.

Roughneck

I went to work on a rig
in the patch
slapping steel
outside Wamsutter
the Red Desert of Wyoming
I the "worm" the
new guy
I stood on a steel mesh floor
at the foot of the 100-foot high tower
and looked out at the snow and
antelopes
and thought of the song "Home on the Range"
sung in 3rd grade
"wake up!" the operator shouted
and a 50-foot long pipe came at me
I caught it
in my gloved hands
and walked across the floor
and positioned the end of it
over the "hole" where
it was screwed into the
previous pipe placed
and sent down the shaft
it was not a job to day dream at
the steel did not give a shit
for flesh
a pipe came fluttering

like a knuckle-ball
in the wind
I caught it in the crook of my arm
and the thing dragged me
across the floor
and clanged against the pipe stub
sticking out of the hole
my little finger in between
split open like a crushed grape
the boss of the rig, the "pusher" looked at the finger and
threw the hand from him, disgustedly
and I got a ride back to town
to the doctor who
sewed me up
and I was glad
that
I still had
ten fingers.

The Minutemen

the varsity needed a defensive back
so I was sent from
the Freshman team to the
varsity scrimmage
the first play a screen pass
I read
and ran in
intercepted the ball
I felt pretty good
about myself
the head coach
up in his tower
high above
bellowed at the quarterback
"do not throw the ball if it is not open!"
I got back into position
at corner-back
the split end a guy only a little bigger
than me
he ran past
like a bullet
and caught a touchdown pass
in front of me
and on the next play
he did the same
I ate his dust
pass after pass

like he and the quarterback
were playing catch
I heard the coach ask
"who is that out there?"
I wanted to hide
disappear
the end zone not dark enough
I ran back to the freshman
afterward
as only a shadow of
my former self.

From DIFLUCAN

Max

I got a room in the YWCA
which was immeasurably better than
sleeping outside
on a bench in the park through
the Y was not without problems,
like the roaches who
came out at night
and ran across my face
I tried to sleep with my mouth closed
but woke one night
after a tickling in my throat
and swallowed a roach
who started to walk around
inside of me
I could feel it
and would punch myself in the belly
and people probably thought I was funny
but I never could kill it and
finally
I went to see a doctor
and was given some pills
I took
but stopped after
over-hearing some trees talking
about me
I drank some CLOROX
to kill the roach

but only made myself ill
and went to the hospital
and had my stomach pumped
(I hate that)
and still the roach
I could feel it kicking
and getting bigger
and I decided to cut it out
and bought a knife
for twenty dollars
but
before I cut
the thing came out
suddenly,
a healthy seven-pound boy
with little roach-face
and two adorably cute antennae.

Rusty

I thought I was hearing some Indian guy
chanting
saying his prayers, the
way they do
Om...Om...
kind of a murmur
louder and louder
until I woke
thinking wtf?
And got up
out of bed
and went to the window
and down below
about fifty yards or so
an orange truck, and
some guy
running a chain saw--
what the Christ!
I stuck my head out the window and
screamed
HEY!
And they looked up
one jerk waved
and they kept it up
tossing branches into the bed of the
truck and
I shouted HEY!

But they did not even look, ignored
me like
I was not there
like I did not exist
like maybe I was a piece of shit, and
I tell you
I was pissed, pissed...
I had not slept more than two hours
or something like that
all night
and what gave them the right
I ask you
to wake me
or anyone! At six AM! And
break the city noise ordinance besides?
How rude and obnoxious
I stuck the barrel of my rifle
a 30.06
out the window
and
just to scare them
fired a shot over their heads
only
FUCK
I missed
and shot the guy in the head
and he dropped
and I thought, hell
no use stopping now
and I shot the guy who

went to the first guy's side
and then I shot the girl
standing by the truck's gate
(another head shot)
and the other guy
who had dropped the chain saw and
hid behind the truck
I could not get a bead on
and put a few rounds into the engine block
to try and flush him
but he stayed put
until
as I reloaded
he made a run for it
and
in the old days
I tell you
I would have got him
but I was rusty, see
and led the fucker a cunt-hair too much
the lucky prick
and, yeah
you might say that
I over-reacted a little
and maybe even that
I was wrong, dreadfully wrong
but
who are you to say anything
to me?
You wake me at

6 AM. on
a morning after I have not slept
and before I have had my coffee
and see what you get
you son-of-a-bitch.

Happy Birthday

I get woke this morning
by a loud bang
sounds like a frag grenade;
I get up
on the wrong side of the bed,
it is my birthday
(hooray)
at Rite-Aid where
I go to get my meds
I tell a clerk to go and
soak her head
after she calls me "Sir"
one too many times;
on the way out
some punk
bumps me
and I give him an elbow
and he say's "what the fuck?"
and I say's "what the fuck what?"
and he shuts-up
lucky for him
I am ready to rip his head off,
I don't know what possesses me;
I go into the bagel shop
which smells like burnt-something
and order from a slant-eyed Asian girl
who takes

like
half an hour to serve me--
I am getting pissed again
and see two cops
at a table
and I say's to the girl
"smells like pork in here"
but she does not respond
maybe does not hear
one of the cop's stares
and I say's "what are you looking at, Porky?"
and he say's "what did you say?"
and I say's "you heard me, I don't stutter."
"You got a problem?" he says.
"Yeah—you."
They get up, walk over to me
the bigger one say's "let's go outside."
He looks just like my 1st sergeant
in the NAM
(a gung-ho mother)
"What, you think I am stupid?" I say's,
and he grabs me, or
I grab him,
I don't know which--
things go haywire quick
everything suddenly loud and
fast, too fast
for me to catch-up with;
I cut-out,
a blackout

a total blank
and
do not come-to again
until in a cell
I wake
inside of
my face in a puddle
of sticky dried blood…
"Happy 65th!" I say's to myself.

Raccoon

Pee Wee football practice over
and
I waited
under a streetlight
at the entrance to the field
for Gramp to come
pick me up
but he did not
and it got dark
then darker
the black silent night
the mountain in front of me
the purple sky
I climbed high up into a roadside tree
and watched a car
its red and yellow lights
go past
and stop
down the street
and I heard the car doors shut
and a voice
"look! It is a raccoon!"
And from out the shadows
a stone
that flew past my head
and then the door of the house shut
as the people went inside

and I climbed down
and stood
at the roadside
my useless helmet in my hand
waiting
until Gramp arrived,
a sheepish smile on his face
a mumbled apology.

Bat Man

no one wanted to be a dirty Jap or
Kraut
except Dicky Heller who
wanted to be
Kraut
because he was German
and his uncle had been in the S. S.
Dickie had a German Luger replica and
helmet he kept on his desk
in his bedroom, the
rest of us were
Americans, Army, Navy, Marines, Green Beret
we fought it out in the woods and
died ten times a night
but always came alive
for the next fight, only
Stevie Heney never
died, not
even after shot point-blank
"you missed," he would say
and dance away
or
"I shot you first!"
He pissed us off and
some started to plot
his real demise or
something like it and

he must have got word
because he stopped coming
around and
stayed home at night and
watched Bat Man
on TV.

Gold

my Uncle tells me to go
upstairs
run!
Bring back his bowling shirt
white with gold letters
yes master
right away
but I hesitate
and feel the pinch of his fingers
like pliers on
my earlobe
and am led around the
kitchen table
a kind of dance
not a waltz
a tango
of pain
that does not go
away when he
let's go
I carry it with me
up the stairs
and back down
through the years
the gold of the shirt
staining my hands
and nothing I could or
can do
to get the stain out.

R. I. P.

Coach Gains, aka "Ripper," bear-like and
with a beer gut and mashed-face
stands in the center of the circle
the woods around the field dark
the mountain behind him
shaped like the Liberty Bell--
we sit on the soft grass
football helmets in our laps;
Coach Gains' gruff sepulchral voice
clear as a bell as he tells the
story of the "dirty player," a guy
whom Coach played against in
Semi-Pro ball; a guy who kicked and
punched and even bit in the pile-ups';
a guy "Ripper" vowed to get, and did
driving his helmet into the guy's gut
once, twice, three times, like a pile-driver
until the guy collapsed and had to be
carried off the field then taken to the
hospital where...he died.
"Let this be a lesson to you boys; play
hard, but play clean! No dirty stuff!"
Cigarettes of coaches and fathers glowed
like fire flies; stars shone, and somewhere
six feet under, lay the dirty player, killed by
Ripper, who, during the day, drove a truck
for the Highway Department.

Eclipse

I was in the fourth grade.
There was an eclipse of the sun coming that
Charlie Baguette and me
agreed to watch
using his father's telescope
(taking turns holding a green welding glass
up before the lens).
On the day of the eclipse I walked across the
backyards, the
day preternaturally bright
the hot grass smelling
like broiled vegetation
to Charlie's house and
knocked…
His mother stood in the screen window
squinting at me
one eye closed,
she wore a pink negligee:
"is Charlie home?"
"No, he is not."
Her breasts popped out of the
pink cups.
"Can I have a drink of water?"
She opened the door only wide enough for
me to squeeze through.
The house smelled like sweat and
something else.

When she turned and stepped to the sink
I shoved my hand up between her legs and
she said, "hey!"
I reached and grabbed the nipple of the
nearest breast;
she spun around, and
I thought I would be slapped but
she grabbed my head and
pulled me to her chest.
I sucked on the nipple and
jammed my hand down the
front of her bikini pants and
started to finger
her snatch.
She moaned and her eyes
went blank
like stars,
no one home.
She said, "oh my god" and
sank to her knees.
She pulled the wiener out of
my shorts and
snapped it up like a fish
taking a bait.
I heard Charlie's footsteps.
"Ma!" he shouted. "What are you doing?"
"Shut-up!" she said. "Go to your room!"
Charlie turned and walked off
in a huff
and I forgot all about the eclipse.

Ice Cream

A maple walnut ice cream cone
10-cents
at Eileen's Dairy bar
where Rose
a teenage waitress
Eileen's daughter
tall and slender,
"a rose yet to bloom"
I told Johnny Garibaldi
who had asked what I thought
of her
the words coming unbidden from
my lips
he blabbed it
and I regretted many times over
a rose yet to bloom
shouted on the street
on the school bus
I stayed away from Eileen's until
desperate for an ice cream
pistachio, butter pecan, black raspberry
I put my thin dime
into Rose's hand
and she did not say
anything
except
"thank you."

Sweat & Leather

Mr. Goldberg with a cigar in his mouth
and a line of tattooed numbers on
his arm
clomp-clomped in his boots
through the new shoe smell
with a box
full of tissue paper
and two shoes
for me
to try on;
I walked back & forth
over the carpet
as my grandmother watched
with a frown
eyeing the price tag
on the box:
"I want these," I said as
Mr. Goldberg chewed his cigar.
Grandma flung the price tag from her
as if hot
and she sent Mr. Goldberg back for
another box from
the dark corridor
where grew the shoes
of sweat & leather.

Puke

one summer we drove 2000 miles
me and two others
in a Volkswagen Beetle
looking to find and pick psilocybin mushrooms
which we found in a pasture
on a back road
in Florida
led there by
a guy we'd met in a bar
who took us to his trailer
and brewed some mushroom-tea
we each drank a glass of
before we three headed back
to the rest area we stayed at
and on the way
the guy in back
puked
into an empty Styrofoam cooler
then asked, "what do I do now?"
and I turned to look at him
and he looked at me
and he lifted the cooler and drank
and when done
he said "don't ever tell anyone," and
I said "I won't," and
never did
until now.

Streetlights

we used to stand in front of the
library
on Friday and Saturday nights
wearing our football jackets
red & white
lightening bolts down the sleeves
like stripes
we said, "I shit you not," and
hocked gobs of spit
onto the sidewalk;
we said—whenever asked if
we had a date, "my name is in the
phone book."
We watched cars go past, some
with a guy and girl inside, and
we imagined where
they were going
but not why
and we spat
and watched the streetlights come on, watched
the stars come out;
we said, "let's do something!"
Said, "like what?"
We never went into the library except
to take a piss or
else
follow some girl inside.

Linebacker

we walked in the woods on
a moon-lit night
a grove of trees
leaves crunching underfoot;
a bunch of us
guys
and one girl
and Starsky, a curly-haired runt
his face upturned
worm-lips moving:
"go get her," he said
and gave me a shove--
she had long blonde hair
silver in the moonlight and
walked by herself
upright
like the trees;
"get her," Starsky commanded, "do it!
You are a linebacker!"
She walked closer then past
and as if
not even seeing us.
Starsky poked me again, the
little prick; he
died that summer
in a car
that crashed and flipped onto

railroad tracks--
I was in the pool room the
morning after when
Fat Molloy came in and
announced, almost gleefully,
"Starsky is dead!"

Geek

I moved up in the right lane
to pass a big truck
on my left
but the truck sped forward and
I floored the Cadillac to get
in front, before the
two lanes became one--
and I moved to the left
and stopped at the light
and the truck squealed to a halt
beside me; the
driver barked down through the
open sun roof:
"YOU FAT BASTARD!"
"Fuck...You," I said.
"Say that to my face!"
I looked up:
"get fucked!"
He swore a blue streak, the
words raining down on me, the
truck engine growling;
I reached into my pocket:
"I will call the cops!"
(An empty threat as
I did not own a cell phone)
I watched him get out of the cab, jump
down

a big muscled-up geek, nickname of
"Moose."
The light blinked green and
I made the turn, glad
we had not come to blows
though
that "fat bastard"
hurt.

Slip

It was Veteran's Day and
although I am not a vet
(my father was)
I decided to celebrate with a drink
or two
even though
I was on probation and
not supposed to drink alcohol.
I went out to a bar where
I got loaded and
became insulting, asking
a guy if he was with his girl or
his dog; calling
a waitress a "dumb bunny" and
interrupting a conversation between two girls and
when ignored, telling
them to go finger each other, which
got me thrown out
but I was not done
and on my way out
grabbed a guy by his collar and
yanked him off his stool
and found myself in the middle of a pile-up of
people
I had to fight my way through
to the door
and out

onto the sidewalk
where a siren I had already heard
grew louder
and I started to run
like a bastard
down an alleyway
and off the top of
a stonewall and
dropped into the
river, cold as ice
and swam to the bridge
and hid in the shadow
I started to climb out
up the stonewall, but
lost my grip and
fell back into the
drink and
got scared
I had to get out
or freeze
I started to climb again
my numb hands
the cold rock
almost to the top
the hands would not grip the
wall collapsed and
I landed back in the icy stew
I started to yell for help and
the lights in an apartment building
over the river

someone shouted down
a man and woman
with a rope
they threw down and
hauled me out, the
woman asked if she
could help and
I asked her to go out with me
and she said "no"
and I walked away
over the snow-covered sidewalk and
toward my room
in a rooming house, my
shoes squishing with each step.

Suspect

I returned to the apartment
at midnight
after the last shift of
my work week
and got out
of the car
my sore legs and feet
the little Shih-Tzu dog
in the next apartment
began to bark at me
from an upstairs window
and I bent, picked-up
a rock and
threw it
and heard the window glass
break
and shards fall
with a sound like chimes
and a light came on
and I ran
around the house
climbed the stairs to my place
and sat
in the dark
listening to excited voices
next door
while watching for cops

who never came
and I went to bed
but before I fell asleep
that goddamn dog
started to bark
again.

Larry

My friend Larry's obituary was not in any
major newspaper;
he was a little man
anonymous
a home-town creation,
part owner of a granite shed who
one night
pulled another man out of
his, Larry's, ex-wife's bed
and when a cop
arrived
Larry picked up a shot gun
and pointed it at the cop
who pointed his pistol
in response
and in the stand-off
Larry said, "if you shoot me, I will shoot you"
and Larry's relatives
who had gathered
shouted at the cop:
"shoot! Shoot him!"
But the cop, a rookie
was shaking too much to shoot
straight
and nobody died
that night
and Larry got off with probation

plus
six months to serve
instead of the years
he could have got
and maybe deserved
for aiming a gun
at a cop.

From ESCAPE FROM THE PLANET CROUTON

Polio

Charlie Baguette's brother Davy
who had polio
used a crutch;
he stood by the porch and
played 45s on a record player
as Charlie and I stripped the
thorny pulp off horse chestnuts
and put the ebony nuts into
a brown shopping bag and
threw the nuts that night
Halloween
at the Camel's house across the street
until cops came with their shiny blue
light and
we ran
into the backyard shadows--
the Camel's thought themselves better than
us, and were mean too
like the German Shepard they kept chained
in their yard:
Davy played Running Bear
Loved Little White Dove
(with a love that never died).
It was the beat of the tom-tom
had set Charlie and me on the
war-path.

Palmer Method

we studied penmanship in school, wrote
long lines of 'c's
like waves coming to shore
and 'e's like little heads;
Miss Good, 3rd grade teacher
blind as a bat and
batty
beat our knuckles with a ruler
then loved us up afterward
with her smothering lilac-scented
flesh; she
lived alone in a brick house
wore a red dress or
else green
one day she broke her yardstick
over Jimmy's shoulder
and the broken half clattered to the floor
and we all laughed and
laughed.

100 pounds

my Uncle the fat mama's boy
collapsed one night
on the porch
and was taken to the hospital with
heart attack
and
afterward went on a diet
began to exercise
lost one hundred pounds
and went unrecognized by
those who knew him, and
then, age 35
he got married and
moved out of the house
and
I was free
of his rules that changed like his moods, of
his back-handed slaps, of the
stench of his B.O., of the
stare of his dark eyes, brown
not blue
like mine.

Prepositioned

to, is, and, if, but
the prepositions of grammar school
rendition,
how about THEN and THAN and
WAS and WERE?
The teacher explained usage but
I did not get it:
got YOUR and YOU'RE
THEIR and THEY'RE but
not then/than
or was/were
I do not think the
teacher knew
any more about it
then/than I did
but she the one
flunked me, told
my grandparents
I was/were slow
which was /were news to
them/there and
suggested I be put into
SPECIAL CLASS
which
back in them/thar days
WAS/WERE called
RETARDED.

Farm

HE HE, HA HA
THEY ARE COMING
TO TAKE ME AWAY
the radio played
the song on the
ride home from
Sand Springs
the aqua-blue pool
in Williamstown, Mass.
the VILLAGE BEAUTIFUL
Gramp with a smile
on his face ha ha
he he his hand on the
steering wheel of the
big Buick; I wondered
what he found funny,
I hung my arm out the
window and
Grandma, in the middle
crabbed YOU WANT TO
GET YOUR ARM CUT OFF?
And I said YES but
pulled it back in;
I heard my brother and
cousin in the rear both
shout BEAVER after
spotting a station wagon

from the rear window
(first to ten BEAVERS won)
it was a half hour drive
home
to the funny farm
in
Adams.

Van Gogh

was a restless kid
his mother a cold
fish
his father, a parson of
respectability;
Vincent was sent to boarding school
he liked home better
and kept returning
like a bad penny
nobody could stand his moodiness
for long
his parents kicked him out
he became a tin Jesus
and went to suffer
with the miners
who thought him a fool
he started to make paintings
after his brother began to pay him
a salary
his parents tried to have him
committed
he moved with the speed and
confusion of
a young Rimbaud
who went to Paris also
like Vincent, two
years in Montmartre

with Theo
before he blew town
for Arles
in the South
16 hours by train
a yellow house
blue moods
and Gauguin
too cool a cat
watched the breakdown
that had been coming
since Brabant
the nut house beckoned
the starry night
the therapeutic baths
the news from Paris and
the Netherlands
and the paint
the paint
on canvases
and the light
lambent
bright
yellow as a heaven
ever could be
purple
in majesty
blue fathom of
sea
and sky

and twinkling eyes
for posterity…
then escape from the loony bin
to Auvers
where the stars went out for Vincent, where
Gachet the Alienist
magician
without magic
played his bit part…
Vincent's new door-sized
canvases
like portals so
vast
and deep
with emptiness
nothing could fill them
but eternity.

Pollock

came out of the West
a mama's boy who
hung-on apron strings
never cut
he became a child of the
alcoholic NYC night
his brothers took care of him
as did Benton's wife
(and the W.P.A.)
and other women who
mothered him
and then his wife
who thought he could do no wrong
she promoted him
and he became
phenomenon
perhaps the greatest painter
in America
sneered LIFE magazine
perhaps not
he did not know
himself
chump or champ
after all the drips
had dried
he could not break through
again

to anything nearly as creative
as those colorful splatters
he went black & white
then figurative
again
and ever deeper into frustration
and a public-suicide trip
(no one called him on his shit)
that finally succeeded
at sixty mph
the final splatter
(he took someone with him, he
could never stand to be alone)
they buried him six feet under
then pulled a huge boulder over
so that
he could not crawl back up.

Poets

Steinman from Gross Pointe, Michigan
told everyone who asked
that he was from Detroit;
Mahoney from a housing project in
South Boston
made sure everyone he met
knew it;
me a farm boy from a mill-town in the corner of
NW Massachusetts
(embarrassed by that)
we smoked a joint while
we waited for the #10 bus
the streetlights of Boston
glaring--
cans of Budweiser in our pockets--
Mahoney was deaf in one ear and
talked loud enough for everyone on the
bus to hear, but
he did not seem to care;
he was a loud-mouth worth listening to
said things worth hearing
--WRITE ABOUT WHAT YOU KNOW ABOUT--
--A BAD CHILDHOOD IS RELEVANT--
whenever I asked him to read poems
I wrote
he always made two piles--
good and less good

one day he said BIG IMPROVEMENT
and I felt as if I'd won a prestigious award…
Steinman wrote without use of
punctuation, between
words the
white spaces
where
he lived
in pauses,
mysteries
large and vacant, like
the lawns of
Gross Pointe.

Another Day

they find me sitting up
in my chair
on the back porch
mid-afternoon
gray sky
no visitors for weeks
maybe more;
my head back
mouth open
eyes pecked-out by birds
HOLY SHIT, a cop says.
I hear him clear as day
I can see him too, eyes
or no eyes, I am
in the sky
above the old ash tree, seems
I can fly, or
something holds me up, don't
know what, it is odd
like the sun
setting
in the east
red
like the blanket
the cops
throw over my face.

I Write For the Factory Workers

the bums,
the burn-outs
the renegades who
left town and never returned;
the unmarried
the unheralded,
lumpen and prole who
never made the honor roll
in High School
never were handed a job
or a promotion
or a trophy;
but got probation,
parole,
an eviction notice,
a Dear John letter,
a court summons,
a pink slip,
a knuckle sandwich,
a room in a nut house,
a ride in the paddy wagon,
a jail sentence,
divorce papers,
bad acid,
food poisoning,
herpes simplex,
crabs,

bronchitis,
mononucleosis,
and hang-overs that
lasted for days.

Blow Me

I asked the wife to blow me
she said
blow yourself
I said
I can't
she said
then get one of your girlfriends to do it
I said
I don't have any you bitch
she laughed bitterly
said
who do you think you are fooling?

I wondered how much she knew and
how she came to know it--
I said
why would I have a girlfriend with you
around, honey?
She said
I don't know MISTER, you tell me.

I hated that MISTER
hated those knee-high boots she
sometimes wore
too
(they always meant trouble for me).

She stamped her foot and
threw her mane of auburn hair around
like a prima-donna racehorse in the gate
at Saratoga
she said
do not think you are getting away with anything
Mister! I can see right through you!

I asked the wife if she was comfortable
she said yes
as comfortable as I can be around you
I said
what does that mean
she said
figure it out yourself
I said
you bitch, I should
she said
should what?
I said I don't know what
she said
how about you should wise-up a little?
I said
how about you should shut-up, a little?
She said
do not tell me "shut-up," who do you
think I am, one of your bimbos?
I said
my BIMBO'S? Oh boy, you have really lost it!
She said

you think?
I said
yeah, you are gonzo, way out there…
She said
and how about you? Do you think you are "normal"?
I said
I never said I was
(whatever "normal" means)
she said
it means not you
I said
Oh, it means you though, right?
She said
more so than you.
I said
do you know how idiotic you sound?
She said
me? Oh brother! You are something!
Said
people see through you from a mile away
and you do not even know it!
I said
what the hell you talking about?
She said
wouldn't you like to know?
I said
yeah, I would
she said
I bet you would
MISTER.

Wayne F. Burke's poetry has appeared in a wide variety of publications online and in print. He is author of seven published full-length poetry collections. The most recent, *ESCAPE FROM THE PLANET CROUTON,* published by Luchador Press, 2019. His poem "Prepositioned" was nominated for "Best of the Net." His poem "Max" won Poem of the Year Honorable Mention from *The Song Is... magazine.* A collection of his short stories, titled "TURMOIL & Other Stories," was published by Adelaide Press, NY, 2020. He is currently at work on a hybrid of memoir/novel. He has lived for the past thirty-five years in the central Vermont region, USA.

www.ingramcontent.com/pod-product-compliance
Lightning Source LLC
Chambersburg PA
CBHW030323100526
44592CB00010B/540